Diary of a Cover Girl

Diary of A Cover Girl

~

Breaking the Silence – Breaking the Chains

Brenda Stone Browder

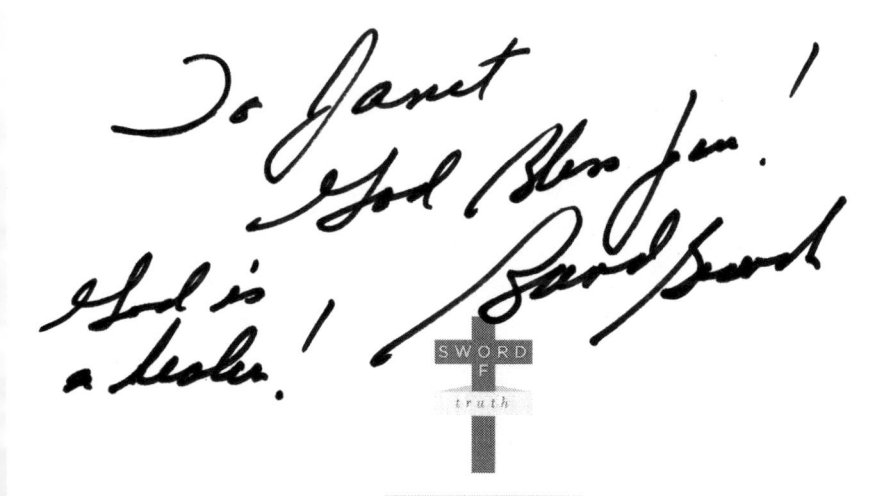

Sword of Truth Publishing

© 2012
Published by Sword of Truth Publishing
Landover, MD

bsb@bendabrowder.com

Printed in the United States of America

All rights reserved no portion of this book may be printed or electronically copied without written permission of Brenda Stone Browder. The only exception is brief quotations in printed reviews.

All scripture quotations are from the King James Version.

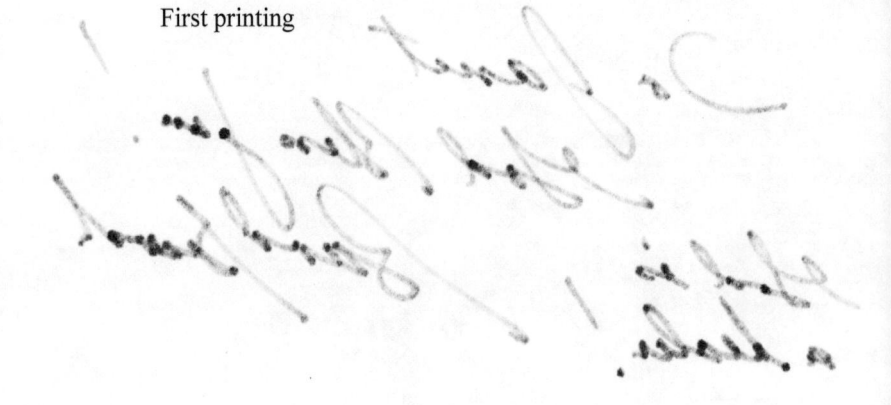

First printing

Dedication

To the women who have "covered" for people in their lives whether their mother, father brother, foster parent, sister, cousin or play cousin, aunt, uncle, niece, nephew, grandparent, employer, child, husband, or minister. Pull the covers off, because the veil has been split, no more secrets to keep us from our destiny!
Break the silence! Break the chains!

~

"I acknowledge God as the lover of my soul the keeper of my life, who supplies all of my needs. Never did I imagine that you would fill the void that plagued me. All that was wrong with my life has been kissed away with your tender love and provision." BSB

~

To my husband, Loren

Before you
I dreamt of having all of the riches in the world
now that you are in my life
having your love and giving you mine
is my ultimate wealth
a reflection of God's love.

~

To my children, Ebony, Brandon, and Loren III thank you for your unconditional love and support, I love you!

~

Forward
By JL King

I am proud of Brenda for becoming the woman that she has become through this journey. Her boldness to speak up and speak out for women, who are still living as "cover girls" because of not knowing what to do or who to talk to, is saving lives. Her ministry of using her own pain and story to show that you can move past the hurt, and walk into your true self is more than most women or men can endure. Her growth as a woman of God and her message of forgiveness is so powerful, and it must be heard.

When I think about her and how long we have been in each other's lives, I smile. I smile because of all the people I know and have met on my journey to acceptance; she is the one person, who never gave up on me, even when my cousins and even my only brother turned their backs on me. That is unconditional love.

Even in the middle of the storms that we both were going through when I came out as a gay man, she still smiled in public and kept her head high. Even when she was hurting and only God could see her pain, in public she still kept smiling and kept her head up high. When she became the joke of the world for not killing me and or cutting off my "penis" as she has been told that some women would have done, she still kept her head up and kept on smiling.

When I was disconnected from my children and they needed a father and not JL King, she kept telling them that he is your dad and he loves you. And she never, not once, made me feel bad. She just stood in the gap and was the mother she knew our children needed.

I could go on and on about Brenda and who she is that a lot of her fans, Facebook friends and even her own brothers and sisters don't know. However, through the pages of this book, you will get to know more about her and who she is.

I have met many women over the past ten years on my journey who have shared their personal stories and most always ask me, how did my ex wife get through. I always answer this question with a simple answer…She prayed her way through. I tell them that she didn't let her hurt overcome her and become a bitter sister whose only purpose in life is to live in misery. She moved on, found a new husband and did her thing. She did not want this short life to be caught up in my mess. She knew that God had a bigger purpose for her life and that our journey was "supposed" to happen to make both of us better people.

To have our "combined" families spend holidays together and to be able to pick up the phone and call her anytime, to talk to her husband and we can laugh and share our roles, as fathers, is truly a blessing to me.

I wish that more couples could get to this place; a place of peace and joy, a place where the past is the past, a place where you embrace today's blessings and not let the past be your present. Life goes on.

In this powerful book, women and men will really get what they need to understand how to forgive and move on, how to use the past to make your future better, how to develop friendships with those who have hurt you, and to understand why God allows that to happen.

I have written fourteen books, spoken to thousands of people around the world, and have had the opportunity to become a household name around the world. I have been blessed, but at the end of the day, and at the end of my life...I would trade all of that to be a better man. I have learned that life has its ups and downs, that life is a daily lesson of how to be a better person. I have also come to a place where I know there will be a better purpose in this last phase of my life. And all of this is because Brenda is still in my life.

As you read her words and feel her true self, know that she is speaking to you from the heart. I am honored to have written this forward for her. I endorse this book as a must read book. I am standing up as a man who understands that time heals all pain, and that this too shall pass.

Thank you Brenda for being "real" and know that I always will have your back.... - JL King

Introduction

God has a way of getting you to the place that will fulfill your destiny. For me God had to move me 500 miles away from what was familiar and comfortable. Had I stayed at the place of my natural birth I would not have fully experienced my new birth in Jesus Christ. I thank God for divine intervention and the strength to listen to and obey the unction of the Holy Spirit's direction, in my life, for such a time as this.

The next chapter, of my life, is not about me; it is about the countless women who have suffered in silence the anguish of living with someone whose selfish motives alter the plans that they know and believe God has for their lives. Many women have found themselves deeply immersed in a relationship with a man who does not have a Christ-like relationship in mind, with no conscious intention of treating his wife as Jesus treats and loves the church.

I left Springfield, Ohio on a journey after receiving prophesies from a woman who was an intercessory prayer warrior in my church.

She approached me, "Why do I keep hearing that you are on unfertile ground?"

My response was awe and shock that she would say those words to me. Knowing that I did not feel a satisfaction, or that I was fulfilling the destiny that God had for my life. I knew God had more in store for my life, more for me to contribute in building God's Kingdom. I was totally unsatisfied, but could not understand why. This woman put clarity on God's call on my life that I was to minister to many women, women who would be delivered from the bondage of living as a "cover girl," by my testimony. God's plan involved living through the test before my desire to live in the Washington D.C. area could be fulfilled. I had the desire when I was a young woman in the late seventies. We relocated back to the United States after my ex-husband's overseas tour in Izmir, Turkey to Texas. I had to wait, wait for thirty-five years for this to be my reality. Through God's sovereignty and providence I am in the DC Metro area living with my present husband Loren Browder; in God's time.

After relocating to the Maryland/DC area and joining First Baptist Church of Glenarden (Pastor John K. Jenkins), I had confirmation that I had arrived at the place that God would have for me. I believed it was of my own choosing. However, God had chosen this place, before my time, at the appointed time.

The producer for the docudrama, New Beginnings pilot, informed me that she would not have proceeded with the pilot had we remained in Ohio. The pilot led to our appearance on a television show, on the *Oprah Winfrey Network's* (OWN) *"Where are They Now?"* in 2013.

    Giving all glory to God, I am compelled to share my testimony to *break the silence and break the chains.*

~

Brenda Stone Browder

PART I

THEN
(Trials that Help us to Evolve to what is New)

CHILDHOOD
(Living in Fear and Shame)

Honor thy father and thy mother: that thy days may be long upon the land which the LORD thy God giveth thee. Exodus 20:12 KJV

Breaking the Silence

I remember school was out for the day I walked up to my house anticipating the smell of dinner cooking. A neighbor kid ran up to me and told me an ambulance had had taken my mother to the hospital. I knew why without asking what was wrong. However, the kid who told me thought that my mother was physically ill when, in fact, she went to the hospital because of her mental illness. She had suffered from what was called manic depression (bi-polar) for most of her life. I wasn't sure if that had been her plight for her entire life; no one would talk to me being the youngest of seven, actually eight children. My family tried to shelter me from the "ugly" parts of life.

My parents' first child, Barbara, passed away at the age of three and was never able to sit up by herself. My father always told the story. My mother never actually talked about Barbara unless my father brought her up. I was told that she had something similar to muscular dystrophy.

I believe my mother never recovered from loosing her first born child and maybe felt a little guilty from that experience. When I informed her that I was diagnosed with multiple sclerosis she said, "I wonder if it was something I did, what did I do to bring this on you and your sister?"

That statement alone led me to believe that Mama thought she was responsible for my illness, and another sister's illness. My sister, Janet, also had multiple sclerosis; she subsequently died of breast cancer at the age of 44; I was 26 when she passed away. Our son, Brandon, had been born weeks prior to her passing. Jimmy and I had lost our twins the previous year.

Mama felt real sorrowful when I told her what the doctor had told me, which I never claimed, because I have always believed that most of our illnesses are 60 percent mental (stress and holding bitterness) and 40 percent physical; our diets directly contribute to our illnesses. We are what we eat.

The day that my mother was picked up by an ambulance I had already learned subliminally from my father to not tell anyone, or to discuss the true nature of her illness with anyone outside of our immediate family. We seemed to feel a shame about her illness; I was too young to understand. I don't think my father understood. He did everything in his power to keep her from sinking into a depression; he did the best he could to cover it up to protect her and his children. I saw her beat his chest and yell and scream at him; all he did was show her love. He never yelled at her, at least not for me to hear. He was a gentleman; he treated my mother like he had treated his mother with love and respect, and taught us to do the same.

Any time there was something major going on in the house, like a relative visiting or when we would take a vacation Mama would, what I called, "shut down." First she would display anger toward someone in particular, mostly my father, and lash out at him over the smallest thing. Then I would notice she would pull at her hair and chain smoke. One time she actually cut her hair really short. Now that scared me because she did something physical to herself, it wasn't just the yelling and uncontrollable rage. Often she would shop and buy the most expensive unnecessary things she could, but those were often items that she really desired.

My older siblings told me that at one time my father put an advertisement in the paper to let the downtown merchants know that he was not monetarily responsible for anything that she had bought at their stores. During that time, the husband was responsible for the bills incurred in the household. I remember a time when she took me downtown and told me she was going to buy me clothes at the most expensive store in our city, a woman's boutique.

I knew she was getting sick because she wanted to shop with no limits. Usually she was thrifty and took me shopping only at the nearly new stores, making sure she did not spend too much money, knowing that we did not have a lot of money; my father worked two jobs to make ends meet. My mother bought my first bra at a thrift store. This shopping trip alerted me that she was on the verge of a "shut down."

She asked me what did I want when we entered the store. I believe she did actually have her own money that day, she still received money from the farm that she and her siblings owned in Kentucky; her father was a landowner and sharecropped part of his 150 acres, they farmed tobacco and sublet the land to other farmers.

Feeling a little apprehensive I picked out a *maxi coat*, a sharp floor-length plaid coat that was made of many colors, and a pair of wide-legged-pants. When we returned home my sister saw our purchases, she was disappointed that Mama bought me something and not her. I felt guilty that Mama spent money on me. Actually, I was afraid not to pick out something, because Mama insisted; I did not want to make her angry, and I needed a winter coat. If we did not get our clothes form the nearly new store we had to make them, all of the girls in our family were excellent seamstresses; Mama also made quilts, as did her mother.

We all learned to tiptoe around mama to not *tick* her off, and were careful not to say or do what we thought would cause her to *go off*. We actually needed more education as to the nature of her illness. It frightened us, mostly because we were afraid that we would grow up to be like her. I remember when the movie *Mommy Dearest* came out, I detested that movie, because I lived in fear much like the little girl in the movie. Mama's personality would change a total 180 degrees when she was ill.

Don't get me wrong when Mama was not "sick" Mama was the sweetest most intelligent person you would ever want to meet, she was polite and likeable. She was pretty too; she loved history and reading. She and my father read the Bible in the living room often together, and they would sing hymns together. She appreciated fine things, and was brought up well, and educated. Her mother was a teacher, as well as, my father's mother. She read to my siblings and me when we were small; she instilled a love for reading in me.

For her entertainment she liked to read *True Detective*, a popular magazine that sold subscriptions and was comprised of short stories, whenever she was not reading about history. She read a lot. I would sneak the magazines them and read them, Mama let us know they were hers and we were not to read them; they were for adults. I believe that is where I get my love for reading books, and my "detective skills."

My mother was fortunate to graduate high school. As a teenager my mother had to live with a white family in the city near her family's farm; since the only high schools were in the city, she had to find a job as a domestic to pay for her room and board while attending school. Leaving her family and living with a strange family had to be difficult for her. There were two young girls in the family; Mama often sadly told me she had to take the two little girls to the movies, on several occasions. Mama had to watch the movie in the balcony and make sure she met up with the girls in the lobby after the movie. My mother experienced living during segregated times. I often wondered if this experience contributed to her instability.

While Mama was at the hospital everyone knew their jobs at home, they were no different than when she was at home. We all pitched in to cook and clean. Mama had taught us how to clean and cook according to our ages. My father's part-time job, as a domestic, and his training as a young man prepared him, he had to step in when his mother took deathly ill when his siblings were small, so he was perfectly capable of running the house when Mama was in the hospital.

The older children would pitch in and take care of the younger and sometimes the younger children would be sent to the Kentucky farm with my maternal grandmother. We would spend weeks at a time with my grandmother and my aunts until my mother recovered.

My grandmother was very strict, as well as, my two aunts; one was a schoolteacher also with high expectations. My nephews and nieces now tease and say it was a "right to passage" to spend time on the farm, we learned additional lessons in manners, poise, and responsibility. I also learned timidity. My grandmother had been a schoolteacher at a one-room schoolhouse, and as I said, was very strict.

I remember one visit with her on the Kentucky farm in particular, she was brushing my hair and I was talking non-stop, I was no more than 6 or 7 years old. I was so excited to be on the farm, and with my grandmother, I was talking and talking. Of course, at that time children were to be seen and not heard.

My grandmother yelled at me to be quiet, "You talk too much!"

I did just that I became quiet and timid. After my grandmother reprimanded me for talking too much and Mama would call me "mealy-mouthed." I didn't say much after that, my little feelings were really hurt from my grandmother telling me that I talked too much. *Our childhood really does shape us; we have to overcome those negative things that were spoken to us or about us.*

Sometimes Mama would decide she did not want to take her medicine; that was when she would get in a "funk." I could always tell when she was getting "sick." The cycle was continuous, Mama would get "sick" and Daddy would take the family on a vacation when she got well, which was stressful for Mama. She would get off schedule with her medicine then she would get "sick."

As long as she took her medicine faithfully she would be okay. She was in the hospital at least once a year when I was small and the stretches in-between became longer as she aged, her illness would exacerbate about every two years.

I remember asking her what were the scars from on her arms; she did not know how they got there. I was later told that the scars came from a time when she was sent to the hospital and had received shock treatments, she was restrained, and struggled so intensely to get free of the restraints that she caused the restraints to dig into her arms causing the wounds. She did not remember because shock treatments cause the patient to loose some memory.

The sad part is our mental health medicine, even in this day, is not too far from this barbaric treatment. We as a society have a long way to go to break the stereotypes of mental illness. The medical community and society have a long way to go to alleviate the notion that mental illness is shameful.

This is how I lived my early years, always tiptoeing around Mama, and keeping the secret. I wanted to leave my parents' home as a teenager so badly to escape being subjected to my mothers illness. I blinded myself to believe that I had two choices: I could have a better life marrying at an early age, or go far away to college. I thought since my parents did not allow me to attend college at Fisk University in Tennessee, because it was too far away, I would rebel.

I was accepted to 3 colleges Fisk University, which was my heart's desire, Wright State University, and Central State University, the family's legacy. Most of my siblings, cousins, and even an Aunt attended CSU. I rebelled against that legacy; I wanted to get as far away from Ohio as I dared. I graduated high school at the early age of seventeen. Tennessee was far enough away and yet close enough to feel secure. My parents said adamantly, "No." So, I decided to attend Wright State, twenty-five minutes from home, instead of Central State, fifteen minutes away, my way of rebelling.

My mother took me to orientation at Wright State, and I was assigned my class schedule and obtained my room assignment. I learned that Wright State was predominately white; Central State was a predominately black school; I came to that realization when the tour guide took me to the "Bolinga Room" where "the blacks" gathered. I learned it was the "Black Student Union." This was during the 70's when black people were fighting for their identity. We listened to songs like Curtis Mayfield and the Impressions' "Keep on Pushin" and James Brown's "Say it Loud I'm Black and I'm Proud." That did not sit well with me at all, to be set apart from the whole student body with a special room in the student union, because I was black. I felt like a fly in a bucket of milk.

After apologizing to my parents I asked them to take me to Central State to enroll which was an historically black university. I had to admit I felt more at home at CSU; I practically grew up on the campus. Four of my older siblings had already graduated from Central State. My parents took me willingly, and did not make me feel bad about making the wrong decision.

I still wanted to get away from my parents home, so I elected to stay on campus at Central State. I was so afraid, since I was the youngest, that I would get stuck at home living with my parents well into late adulthood. I had six siblings; however, I thought I alone would have to continually deal with my mother's episodes, although I loved my mother I wanted to be free from the emotional rollercoaster. I excelled in my major, Spanish Education; my advisor wanted me to be an exchange student in Mexico. Ironically I turned down the offer, I was actually afraid to be that far away from my family. I dropped out of college after a year, I married Jimmy, ironically Jimmy was stationed in Izmir, Turkey and I joined him.

The cycle began again of me keeping family secrets, as I had been taught. I now realize my early years shaped my adult life of keeping secrets and living in denial. I believe that people have a propensity to marry the person whom reflects their parent(s), someone with the same characteristics, however not intentionally. The choice is likely subconscious. I believe I made that subconscious choice; in a sense my mother lived a double life as well as Jimmy.

***

I always knew what my childhood issues were, but I often wondered what were Jimmy's circumstances growing up. I wondered if something happened to him in his youth, for him to have a proclivity to men.

I remember Jimmy's father told me the story about coming home one day when Jimmy was an infant. Mr. King walked into the house and the house was steaming hot. Jimmy's mother had the heat in the house extremely hot because she did not want her baby to be cold, and was making sure he was comfortable. There were blankets piled on top of him in addition to the heat.

His mother had lost several babies they were stillborn. She had taken extra precautions during her pregnancy with Jimmy to insure his survival and was overly protective of him as an infant and little boy. Maybe his mother "smothered" him with her protection.

REFLECTION / DIARY

My childhood shaped me, and the choices that I have made. How has your childhood shaped you and the choices that you have made throughout your life?

REFLECTION / DIARY

MISSING THE SIGNS

"If it looks like rain, it smells like rain, and it is wet like rain, then it is rain." ~ BSB

Jimmy put the wedding ring on my right hand during the wedding ceremony instead of my left hand. I quickly and discreetly put the ring on my left hand praying that no one saw the mistake. Perhaps no one noticed the ring, because of the distraction of his mother's red pinstriped pantsuit, her way of showing her objection. Looking back I was happier during our courtship than in our marriage, and that is because I was in love with love.

I spent an enormous amount of time and thought selecting the items in my trousseau. Jimmy made a comment about my lingerie that I had carefully chosen for our wedding night, "It looks like a shroud." That hurt deep. I had no clue. I should have taken that to be a warning. I was eventually to be the shroud, the cover up, and his cover girl. I should have taken heed to his mother's objection. What I imagined our relationship to be was more than it actually was.

Jimmy sent me greeting cards and letters while he was away in the service, proclaiming his undying love for me, all the while having an interest in men. Looking back I was in more denial than Jimmy. I was actually blinded because I wanted to be in love so badly. He had a nice car, wore nice clothes and nice shoes. My mother used to stress that a man should wear shined shoes. Now, I know what she meant is, are they clean? Whose bed is he putting his shoes under? Yes, I was very shallow and naïve at the same time. A few love songs, a car and clothes, were all it took to woo me.

So really, why didn't I know? I ask myself that question quite often, "Why didn't I know?" The signs were all there for me to see. I would have seen them had I not been naïve, and shallow. Jimmy was the perfect boyfriend we came up in the era of "ooh baby radio." I still have most of his collection of vinyl albums, I gave him a few right after our divorce settlement. I now laugh out loud at that. The nature of our relationship consisted of I love you and there-is-no-other-for-me-what-will-I-do-without-you-I-will-never-let-you-go, kind of love.

~

I will share a "love letter" that I wrote to Jimmy when I was a senior in high school with the help of a friend; it might sound corny to some or maybe you can relate. Remember, even music can shape and influence us in our choices, good or bad, especially young people. Be careful what you put into your mind.

"Life can never be exactly like we want it to be; I can be satisfied knowing you love me. Betcha' by golly wow, you're the one that I've been waiting for forever and ever will my love for you keep going strong. If my lonely heart could speak it could tell you, baby I'm for real. It was right on the tip of my tongue, but I forgot to say 'la la' means I love you.

For your love I would do anything. Show me how. You know I want you how bad I need you. I want to kiss you right now. So come on make sweet love to me. I know you can do it, for your precious love means so much to me. Try me, I could l never love another after loving you. So baby love, come see about me. These are some of the things that make me know we can make it if we try. This is how I feel.

Running away sure ain't gonna' help; I'm gonna' get you. So make me the woman that you come home to, and we'll be always together, just you, just me. Our day will come and we'll have everything, or is this just my imagination running away from me?

Baby you can't blame me; I want to make it with you. Baby, ooh baby, I love for you to call me baby. When you squeeze me real tight you know it makes wrong things right. I can't stop wanting you. I can't stop loving you. If that's not love who is gonna' love me if you walk out that door? There will be no one new 'cause my whole life is you.

You know I told my friends just the other day, whoever would try to take me from you has got to be a foolish fool. My love for you is too strong; we've been together for so long. You see breaking up is so hard to do, and I never can say goodbye.

So you think my hearts made of stone? 'Cause when you're near me there's no reaction, well you're wrong. The touch of you is driving me out of my head. Not on the outside, but inside strong. Hypnotized. You got me going in circles. What am I to do? My mind is in a whirlpool. I can't see you when I want to; I'm like a bridge over troubled waters. For you, I would do anything, just call my name and I'll be there.

I just want to let you know somebody loves you. So, let's stay together; because to me you are everything, and nothing can take the place of you. Sunshine blue skies I give to you with love 'cause, I do love you. The other day while thinking of you I just had to say to myself, God bless whoever sent you 'cause I really need you. There are many ways to say I love you, but any one you use is good enough for me."

p.s. *"Nothing can take the place of you."*

~

Really? Hindsight: I was in love with love, and blind with love. He would not let me go, but he was not going to be faithful either. He wanted to have me, and his gay lovers.

Wake up if you are merely in love with love and not actually in a meaningful relationship, where the love is genuinely reciprocated. My vision was distorted.

I did not see that he spent too much time with his friends during our marriage. Friendship is good, however there are limits and boundaries when you are a married woman or man. Jimmy's friends overstepped those limits and boundaries. One friend in particular was married; he was constantly trying to get me to spend time with his wife while he and Jimmy "hung out." I now know that was a distraction and an excuse for them to spend time together. He spent way too much time with his friends, some that I did not know. I could not understand why he wanted to spend more time with them than me. His friends that he did not bring to the house were flamboyant and obviously gay.

I had demanded that he introduce me to a man who would call the house, whose voice would change from a high pitched sing-song tone to a low baritone. Something did not "feel" right about him. After Jimmy reluctantly introduced him to me it was obvious. The friends that he had were gay, I now know that he enjoyed their company more than mine and why.

Often times a tactic that a man will use to cover up his behavior is to use the character flaws that his wife has, or he will set out to "break" her and create character flaws in her, such as lowering her self-esteem. He will do this with snide remarks, withholding affection, and some use physical as well as mental abuse. This enables him to have control over the relationship.

The reason why I missed the signs in my marriage is simple; he intentionally deceived me and lived the lie like a well-trained actor.

REFLECTION / DIARY

What, if any, signs have you missed in your relationship/s? Write your testimony/story:

REFLECTION / DIARY

FAMILY

Unconditional Love of Family

Family values were instilled deep within me. My family was extremely close, almost cult-like in the aspect that no one was allowed in without approval of the family. We had friends, but not a long list. We had special close friends. My father scrutinized our friends; of course I grew up in a small town so most people knew each other. Our father instilled in us to stick together; he would tell us, "When one is down, everyone is down." In other words we were to stick together. Which was another irony because we had a tendency not to tell each other our true feelings and what was really going on in our lives. I believe we still walked on eggshells not to worry the family, to upset anyone, especially my mother.

I took a long time to tell my parents Jimmy and I had separated, my brothers and sisters knew right away. "Tell one you tell them all." I had a hard time telling my parents that my marriage failed. They had been married for over forty years at the time of my divorce; I felt I had failed their example. My father was disappointed that Jimmy would let his sexual desires override his loyalty for his family, for my father nothing came before family. He was hurt because he knew his baby girl was hurting.

My mother's reaction came from her upbringing that you stand by your man and keep your family looking like a god-fearing upstanding family, perfection on the outside. She wanted me to allow Jimmy to live in the small suite on the back side of our house, and come and go out of the back door, avoiding interaction with me. She came from a place that she lived – her mother and father eventually did not live in the same house, but on the same land. My grandfather moved to a small house meant for hired help on their land. He and my grandmother just did not get along, I was never told anything further about their physical separation, they did not divorce; divorce was unheard of during those times. My mother was sad about our break-up but she did not believe that Jimmy was betraying me with men for a long time. She wanted me, as her mother did, to pretend to the community that all was well.

My siblings came to bat for me, but were actually torn because they had such a fondness for Jimmy; and still do; he had and still has a charismatic personality. My oldest brother was protective of his baby sister, as he still calls me, and was totally upset about his little sister being hurt. He somehow got into a heated argument with Jimmy's mother and cousin, which ended with a lot of animosity between our families.

I was not around at the time of this heated exchange, however I felt the repercussions from Jimmy's mother's coldness toward me. I couldn't expect anything less from a mother protecting her son. She and Jimmy plotted together to deem me an unfit mother in the courts; they were being vindictive.

Jimmy's father would often say to me, "I'm hurt. Jimmy messed up!" He would not talk to me about the real reason for our breakup; he was in denial, nor did his mother. I see now why Mrs. King was so adamant about us not marrying in the beginning. Mother's know their children.

We eventually became cordial toward each other, after she and Jimmy realized the battle was futile and unfounded, and not good for our children. I was not trying to keep the children away from either of them.

After the children were older she would call me just to talk. Jimmy's father would often stress to me that I would always be a part of their family, that he would always love me.

My family was more accepting of our divorce than Jimmy's family, maybe it was because once they understood the circumstances they were ashamed. I believe my family learned to accept people through our relationship with our mother and her illness, we learned early in life how to love unconditionally.

Jimmy asked me to change the routine that we had gotten to a science for his visitations with the children, in Columbus, Ohio where he lived after our divorce; Columbus was about an hour away, it made since for us to meet halfway between Columbus and Springfield. We were being cordial meeting half way for the visits. We would set a time when we would meet at the truck stop. I would pack the kids up, unwillingly, take them to the truck stop and he would meet me there to gather them and their weekend belongings, or their summer load of clothes. I detested when they would have to go for their extended stays, but I needed to let them have time with their father, I knew then how much he loved them. I did not want them to hate me for not allowing them to have visits with their father. The truck stop was safe and non-threatening for the both of us.

Those were the times when it was quite awkward for Loren and Jimmy to be in eye-view of each other, nor did Loren want him to come to the house and Jimmy did not feel comfortable with that either. Especially after Jimmy had pulled off one time with me still leaning in the window of his car and I was pregnant with Loren III. Loren wanted to hurt him. Jimmy and I were not in agreement on an issue involving the kids and child-support. I now know I should not have had those conversations with him. I should have let the courts speak for me.

I strongly urge couples experiencing difficulties in their marriage to seek counseling from a professional. Sharing with friends and family will give you the support that you need. However, they most likely will be partial to one or the other party. I also urge couples to try to work out their differences before deciding to end the relationship, often times the pain of betrayal is so deep that things are said and done in anger.

I thank God that we are no longer in that place of anger and bitterness. We are now living in the benefits of forgiveness.

REFLECTION / DIARY

Family was and is extremely important in my life. How has your "family" supported you?
Family: People who support you, who are related to you through bloodlines or your organic support group.

Brenda Stone Browder

REFLECTION / DIARY

PART II

NOW

(New – Old = Wisdom)

CHANGED FOREVER

Therefore if any man be in Christ, he is a new creature: old things are passed away; behold, all things are become new. 2 Corinthians 5:17 KJV

The Oprah Winfrey Show

Admittedly I was upset the first time Jimmy went on the Oprah show. Jimmy was being glorified and my life had been hell. I wanted to be asked how did I feel, I wanted her to have the conversation with me, his ex-wife, and not have him speak for me, or about me without my presence. Was this not a show for people (women in particular), for them to be empowered, to have their say? Why was I not asked to be on the show? All of these questions were milling through my head. I wanted to scream loud enough into the television so someone would hear my voice, my stifled voice. I later learned that J had told the producers that I was not ready to be on the show.

As I watched the show I reflected on the conversation and my thoughts, on that day when Jimmy had spoken with my daughter and me a couple of years prior:

J's face was serious as he sat in his immaculate home, going the extra mile to make my daughter and I comfortable. "Would you like a drink Brenda; what can I get you Ebony?" He seemed to be stalling for time. My thoughts were, "He is finally going to tell our daughter, in my presence, about his lifestyle. I thought, "Now I can live easy, not obligated to keep J's secret any longer." Skirting around the true reason why her parents were no longer married was becoming more and more difficult the older the children became.

> I thought, "I know why you called us here, you are going to finally come clean about breaking up our home, let's hear it, and be gentle with our daughter. Go ahead tell her you sleep with men, I won't have to protect you any longer."
>
> It was more and more difficult to hide, especially around relatives. They wanted to have conversations in code when my children were around or make snide remarks. The children were mature now and I thought, "J it's time, let it out tell our daughter the truth, tell me the truth." I wanted to hear it from his mouth. Years had past since our divorce, it was time to move on to the next stage. Finally he did just that, subtly at first, speaking as if he were describing someone else's life.
>
> "There are men who have sex with men and I am speaking out publicly on this issue because it is hurting families, women, and children both emotionally and physically...our lives are about to change forever..."

As I sat alone in my family room watching The Oprah Winfrey Show I recalled the conversation that Jimmy and I had with our daughter. Wiping the wetness off of my face to see the television screen clearly when my daughter came into view, my tears stopped. I focused on Oprah's words as she directed questions to my daughter. My daughter! I wanted to protect her again as I did when she was a child. But, I did not need to, Oprah was kind with her questions, and it was obvious that Ebony was a grown woman and could hold her own.

Jimmy and I were at the brink of hating each other, then snapped out of what seemed like a nightmare. During our eight-year marriage my biggest fear (wives and women in relationships can confirm the magnitude of the biggest fear) was that I could not hold the interest of my husband, that he would loose interest and let his attention and heart wander. I feared that he would engage in extramarital affairs with women. Well, I was wrong he did not betray his love for me, with women, he betrayed me with illicit affairs with men, one in particular. Not only did he betray me, he let the whole world in on his escapades via his book, On the Down Low, and through his public speaking. The ultimate was when he spoke on the most widely watched television show, *The Oprah Winfrey Show*. "How could this be happening to me, is it something that I have done?" I asked God, as I watched the show in my family room alone and wounded.

The show aired on the east coast first. I actually watched through a semi-conscious mind at my brother's house with my family. They made comments throughout the whole show, I could not focus nor could I, or would they engage in my need for a wet emotional cleansing. I viewed the show while actually tuning out the show, my family, and my thoughts. I decided to leave and view it later on the west coast channel, later at home – alone. The same way I felt throughout the years, alone. No one else could possibly have lived this same lie, were my early thoughts.

I have found out differently after the controversial public disclosure of my ex-husband's sex life. Numerous women have bombarded me with their stories of infidelity and extramarital affairs involving their boyfriends and husbands. They too speak of feeling alone until the disclosure of the down low phenomena.

Our lives had, in fact, changed forever.

The disclosure of our private lives in public made a difference in the smallest portion of every day living: While shopping for groceries my life became open for discussion; invariably when I stepped out of my car to shop at the local grocery, someone would say hello then, I knew it was coming, *"I saw your husband on Oprah."* They wouldn't refer to him as my ex-husband. I was still associated as Jimmy's wife, and people in the community had seen me with my husband, Loren, for years.

I had to re-live the past when Jimmy was thrown in the public eye. The sensationalism of his secret life made people think that our divorce had just happened. The divorce had been final for years however, the public disclosure, healing and forgiveness had just occurred.

Some would boldly ask Loren, how does that make you feel? Loren would answer, "That does not make me feel anything, she is married to me now. Early on in our marriage Loren protected me from Jimmy's jealous antics and vengefulness. He became my protector even more, shielding me; and reminding me not to worry about what people say or think.

Loren and I both gave up the typical lifestyle that he and I were used to, going to the park and church on Sunday. We were thrown into a different arena, semi-celebrity status (in my hometown), I say semi because Jimmy was the New York Times best-selling author, and I just happened to be his ex-wife, until…until I got a call from him expressing that people wanted to hear from me, they wanted my story. He asked me to write a book with him about our marriage; initially I was reluctant to write my story with him. However, I explored the idea.

He put me in contact with his co-writer, Karen Hunter. I was able to connect with a publishing company through Karen, after some failed negotiations with Jimmy to write with him. Karen had my back and kept me from making some bad publishing decisions. She found an editor who was very much interested in hearing my story not Jimmy's story; she had already heard his story.

Karen Thomas, then an editor at Kensington Publishing, had just read Jimmy's book and saw him on Oprah and wanted to know about his ex-wife. "What happened to her?" Subsequently I did not co-write with Jimmy. With Karen Hunter as my co-writer and Karen Thomas as my editor we published <u>On the Up and Up: A Survival Guide for Women Living with men on the Down Low</u>, which became an Essence Bestseller.

The book was difficult to write. However, I was in the process of writing my story in fiction prior to Jimmy being on the *Oprah Show*. Writing in fiction would prove to be relatively easy, but to write my story in non-fiction where I became the first-person-main-character was quite difficult. During my writing sessions with Karen I would actually tremble while giving her an account of the scenarios of my life with Jimmy, and how I found out that he was sleeping with men. The book was published strategically one year after Jimmy's book.

My *life had changed forever*; the book catapulted me into numerous book signings, radio interviews, television talk shows, and conferences. I interviewed for Ed Gordon on NPR; I was on the Montel Williams Show, CNN, and Inside Edition. Also some local television shows. I traveled from one end of the United States to the other and Bermuda.

REFLECTION / DIARY

Have you had an experience in your life that has tested your faith and trust, changed you forever, and shaped your life's story? Have you overcome, moved on from your test, and allowed God to make this your testimony? (Read Proverbs 3:5-6)

REFLECTION / DIARY

Brenda Stone Browder

THE JOURNEY OF REDEMPTION

I had befriended a woman in Bermuda at a conference, *The SisterSpeak Health Spa Getaway*. The conference was presented by the *Black Women's Health Imperative* and sponsored by *Ebony Magazine and NBA Basketball Wives*; I was one of the speakers. The woman whom I had befriended during the conference was engaged in a serious relationship with a man in a prominent position. We kept in contact after the conference. She later discovered that he was also involved in a relationship with a man; he was on the down low. She told me she was distraught when she discovered his secret, but found herself better prepared for this reality after she had heard my story. God's providence prepared her for what was to come. This is why I truly believe nothing is by accident.

During that conference, I met several wonderful ladies who also spoke at the conference, including Melba Moore. Her performance in her one-woman show, *Sweet Songs: A Journey in One Life*, taking us through her life and loves was phenomenal.

The speakers' shared stories created a bond, which carried us into the evening on the second day of the conference when we were treated to a festival and a Patti LaBelle concert held at a band shell by the sea. (Imagine my awe at riding in a taxi on the island of Bermuda with an entourage, which included Melba Moore, and dining together at the festival!) The jazz violinist set the heaven-like tone to the evening. What a wonderful performance engulfed by the evening sea breeze!

Ironically I had referenced Patti LaBelle's book, <u>Don't Block Your Blessings,</u> in my book. To feature my book at the conference and to be able to see Patti LaBelle in concert in Bermuda was surreal! I said a little prayer to God, "Thank you God for using my testimony to bring clarity to some and healing to others, and thank you God for blessing me with this awesome evening." I felt as though God was saying, daughter here is one of those blessings that you did not block – an evening in paradise.

Ebony magazine featured a story on the conference; amazingly I was mentioned in the article. My picture was actually in the magazine!

My parents typically, as most African-American families, showcased the Ebony front and center as a coffee table book. I had bought every magazine since I had left my parents home as a young woman. Did I mention that my daughter's name is Ebony? I also had an extensive collection of the Essence Magazine. I had more copies than the local library. I am now thankful for the online version.

After I had been published in the magazines, I stopped collecting them cold turkey. I had been compelled to purchase every magazine that I could purchase; I can honestly say it was an obsession. I had so many magazines! They physically took over my office space. Maybe I was prophetically purchasing them waiting for my articles to appear in both the Ebony and Essence publications. Well, that was a full circle moment for me. When Loren and I made the move to the D.C. area and downsized I got rid of my collection; it was difficult, but necessary to purge. I used the same process to let go of the magazines as I used to purge my past relationship; it was an emotional process to let go. The

Ebony Magazine sponsored trip to Bermuda to keynote their event was cathartic.

All of my events and book signings did not fair as well as a tropical trip to Bermuda. There were times during my tour with my book and speaking engagements where I faced opposition. Opposition was one thing that I was not initially prepared for, on some occasions I was blackballed by *Lesbian, Gay, Bisexual and Transgender* (LGBT) groups. I had expressed to them my message was not of hate, I wanted them to understand my position. Just like in the 1960's when African-Americans found it difficult to convey that they were not against any certain group, but promoted the rights of African-Americans. I used to say I am pro black, and not against any other race. In the same manner I conveyed to people of the LGBT groups that I encountered I was not promoting negativity against any group, I promote the emotional and physical health of women in relationships. I am against the lies told by some men (and some cases women) who selfishly hide their sexual preferences and practices to their wives and girlfriends.

Women's lives are put in jeopardy, both physically and emotionally. I am concerned for some people who intentionally do not uphold the marriage covenant, living a lie from the beginning of their relationships, who have intent to deceive. My platform comes from the place where I have been, the place of despair, feeling alone, confused, hurt and betrayed. My platform comes from my belief in God's Word. The deceit of a man on the down low does not uphold the marriage covenant. *"Marriage is honorable in all, and the bed undefiled: but whoremongers and adulterers God will judge." Hebrews 13:4*

Through all of the pain and suffering and Jimmy's intent to deceive me for as long as possible, I have evolved. What he did within our relationship will never be acceptable, and I will never forget. He committed adultery; he was a thief and a liar – he stole my love on false pretenses. But, I ask God to forgive me of *my* sins; I am not perfect I too have to crucify my flesh daily. We have both gone through a process, him learning his truth and me learning mine. I have learned to trust in God's truth, allowing God's truth to sustain me.

The Oprah Show, 2010

The truth was revealed about my marriage in the next *Oprah Show,* in 2010. I was not invited to the first show in 2004. However, I was invited to the second Oprah Show in 2010. My full circle moment was when I got the call from a Harpo producer. He expressed that they were re-visiting past shows that had made an impact on the *Oprah Winfrey Show* viewers. The show discussing men on the down low had made an impact. The producer had contacted Jimmy and asked how his life had changed since the 2004 show; he expressed to them that he and I had become cordial. I got my chance to redeem myself on *Oprah*.

Jimmy and I sat in the green room waiting to be called, individually to the stage. He was clowning trying to make me relax, "I just know I'm going to get a car. I can hear her now. You get a car!"

I was shaking as I walked from the green room onto the stage; I was praying that I would reflect the light of God. I was no longer bitter I wanted people to know that you do not have to remain in the bondage of bitterness. I did not want to look bitter. I had just been thoroughly pampered in the makeup room. I knew full well why I was there: however, I was seizing my moment; the make up artist asked me if I wanted false eyelashes, of course I said yes, and she asked me if I wanted to be air brushed. I said, "I want it all." I had learned from the master, Oprah, to "seize the moment." I knew that very moment would never happen again.

I serve a good God! I was restored and redeemed. Although I did not get to speak extensively on my life-changing marriage to Jimmy, most of what I said was edited to a couple of sound bytes, God gave me double for my trouble, not only did I get to share with the entire viewing audience, but to sit next to Oprah was telling someone who really cared about my story; she was compassionate, kind, and flawless. My husband, Loren, was in the audience; looking out at him gave me strength.

Jimmy's <u>On the Down Low</u> gave an account of his escapades and details of his down low lifestyle, a perpetrator reversing the lie and my book, <u>On the Up and Up</u>, gave an account my being a victim to evolving into victory. I hate to call myself a victim; the key is to rise above what has been perpetrated. I had to allow myself to heal and rise to forgiveness. In the beginning I wanted the world to know my story, now I want the world to know how to bring about healing, I want the world to know what that healing looks like. I want the world to know the rest of the story, no longer hurt and no longer hurting. I want men and women in estranged families to know there is life after divorce; you can forgive, heal, and love again. I chronicle and candidly share the process of the journey.

Divorced and separated families, through our example, can move into a blended loving family. No longer a perpetrator and no longer a victim; However, It Takes Two. *Yes, I have forgiven him.*

REFLECTION / DIARY

God will show us through confirmation from events or others if we are walking in His purpose. Has God shown you your purpose?

Brenda Stone Browder

REFLECTION / DIARY

FORGIVENESS IS NECESSARY

"Forgive us our debts as we our debtors"
Matthew 6:12 KJV

Breaking the Chains

People often ask me how can I forgive Jimmy for the lie that he perpetrated throughout our 8-year marriage. I have forgiven him because I know that I ask God daily for forgiveness, merely reciting the Lord's prayer convicted me of my need to forgive Jimmy, Sin is sin, and no sin is greater than any other sin, we all have sinned; that is not a cliché, it is a fact. How can I ask God to forgive me if I cannot forgive others? My forgiveness did not come from me, but through the mercy of God. There is nothing else that could have brought me through this, only the love of God. I look at Jimmy as through the eyes of God, and now the romantic love that I once had for him as a wife has evolved into an agape love for him, through my relationship with Christ. Jimmy is the father of my children and I want the best for him, I wish him no harm.

Forgiveness does not require me to forget. Forgiveness for me did not come overnight there were times when I wanted to have the fortitude to hurt him in some manner, either physically or mentally for what he had done to ultimately destroy our family, and for putting me at risk for any number of sexually transmitted diseases. I am thankful to God that he spared me to share my story, this being the very reason that I have felt compelled to share my testimony with others. God spared me from disease, and from bitterness, thankfully I share my story with others to empower them with knowledge and strength to make responsible decisions in their relationships.

I not only forgave Jimmy I also forgave the man who was in his life that he was having sexual encounters with during our marriage right at our break-up, the man who was sleeping with my husband. This encounter was during an actual church service when I was feeling on top my "holier than thou" game. I was actually sitting in the pulpit with the ministers as a lay leader of the church where I was a member. The visiting minister had preached his sermon on defining moments. He said, "Either you have been through a defining moment, or you are going through a defining moment, or you are about to go through a defining moment." I thought *God is good and I am GOOD, no issues here, I am saved, sanctified, filled with the Holy Ghost, and fire baptized.*

Little did I know that the man, I refer to him as Melvin as I did in my book On the Up and Up, was at the church service. Mind you every time I encountered Melvin in public I would turn my head in disgust and displeasure, daring him to look my way, let alone speak to me. When the church service was over everyone cleared out of the sanctuary, somehow I, and a couple of others remained in the sanctuary. I looked up after walking out of the pulpit and there was Melvin approaching me, of course I started to stare him down and walk the other way. However, I was stopped, God quickened me in my spirit and told me you need to forgive him. I felt that this was my defining moment. (Read *Matthew 6:9-15*)

Melvin walked directly up to me and said, "I need to ask you to forgive me." I said, "I forgive you." We hugged and we cried together, before God. Both of us had been hurt and were hurting. That forgiveness led to healing, in my mental and physical body. I was further able to let go of the hurt and pain and bitterness that I harbored in my heart.

Forgiveness is key, bitterness is the ultimate disease, because it can perpetuate any other disease, your body is not designed to hold stress and it not manifest in some other physical manner. Spirit, mind, and body, all must be in sync. Through that release of bitterness and hatred God healed my body. Some do not want to believe or accept my testimony of my healing of multiple sclerosis, I know what God did for me is real. I had been diagnosed with MS at the age of 35; I experienced numerous tests, and treatments over the years and symptoms would come and go, and increase and decrease, but never left me completely.

The encounter at church with Melvin was fifteen years after my diagnosis, as a routine evaluation a few weeks after our encounter. I had a MRI that my doctor ordered, the neurologist looked at the results and asked me, "I diagnosed you with multiple sclerosis?"

I said, "Yes."

He looked at me puzzled and said; "I see nothing on the results of your test that indicate that you have multiple sclerosis."

I said, "That's God!"

He said, "If that is what you believe I respect that."

PRAISE GOD!

I praise God for not only bringing me out of a

dark marriage and healing my body, but also empowering me to tell my testimony with boldness to encourage and empower others.

This brings me to a story about a man at a church in Wilmington Delaware. I had finished speaking on forgiveness and was leaving the pulpit area when a man approached me and grabbed my hand to help me walk down the stairs, I thought he was placed there to assist the clergy.

He placed a fifty-dollar bill in my hand and said, "This is for you sister; you don't realize how you have helped me understand that I need to forgive someone. Before hearing your testimony I was on my way across country to kill someone. He had stolen all of my belongings out of my apartment, I wanted revenge on him, but now I know that is not the answer, I need to forgive him and move on, thank you sister. This is not enough but I want to bless you."

That was God! I had moments earlier apprehensively put fifty dollars in the offering for the families who had been affected by HIV/AIDS. The ministry had asked everyone attending the service to bring a household or personal item to donate, which I did not have since I had traveled there by airplane.

Not only was the man saved from sinning, the man wanted to bless me with his gift of fifty dollars through God for sharing my testimony. I realized at that moment that my witness would be bigger than my man sleeping with other men.

REFLECTION / DIARY

*Forgiveness is necessary and enables you to move on with your life, and allows God to move you into your purpose. What and who do you need to forgive to be free to live an abundant life? (*Read *Ephesians 4:32)*

REFLECTION / DIARY

MOVING ON

Now unto him that is able to do exceeding abundantly above all that we ask or think, according to the power that worketh in us...Ephesians 3:20 KJV

After the first *Oprah Show* aired Jimmy called me to advise me to move from my hometown. I never wanted to relocate back to Ohio in the first place. It was Jimmy's idea to move to Texas.

When we left Turkey I remember, verbatim, the conversation. I specifically said, "I don't want to move to Texas. Paul lives there and I don't want to move to a city where I know you will ignore me, and spend most of your time with Paul, I can't stand Paul!"

I thought, *"Now you have no say over where I live, my husband and I will decide where we live. You gave up the privilege a long time ago."* I hung up the phone thinking out loud, "You still want to control me, not today, or any other day. It's a new day; I have a new life and a new husband." I wanted to tell him that his friend Paul had called me right after our breakup and asked me to move back to Texas and live with him.

"Who was that on the phone?" Loren asked after my loud conversation with JL.

"Jimmy." I reluctantly told Loren about the conversation.

"Well, you told him right, he does not have any say over what goes on in this house… The kids are grown and in college…if he calls here again with that, let me talk to him."

But deep down I knew Jimmy was only looking out for both Loren and my welfare. He knew the problems he had incurred with the new title of "Mr. DL." He had received threats on his life for disclosing the "secret." I softened up my thoughts, but did not admit to Jimmy, that I had already considered the possibility of moving from our small hometown where everyone knew that my first husband had broadcast to the world, on the

Oprah Winfrey Show, that he had slept with men and that is the real reason for the quintessential couple's breakup.

After the public disclosure of our breakup I no longer had the privacy I once knew. No matter what the conversation of the day was, the topic inevitably evolved to the "down low." It was just like buying a new car you see that same car everywhere.

Watching television sitcoms and listening to the radio, I was constantly reminded of what I wanted so much to forget and move on. And then other times I wanted to have my say and join in on the conversation. Even now while watching television if an African American sitcom is airing you can put your money on the conversation evolving to the "down low," or something similar. Sometimes I would surf the Internet and channel surf looking for information, television shows, and movies that addressed men sleeping with men, and specifically addressed JL King AKA Mr. Down Low.

I was looking for confirmation that I was not crazy in my accusations, that it was a fact. I was not wrong. I did not accuse an innocent man, as my pastor had asked me years prior, "What if you are wrong?"

And like any other hot topic in the news the comedians had a field day. I wondered if we should move away, "Are we the joke of the town?" Loren kept me grounded, and my head held up.

He always told me don't worry about what people say or think, they are always going to talk about you, and have their opinion, and if not you there will be someone else. Loren has a practical-common-sense way of approaching issues. He has a lot of "street" knowledge and a wise no-nonsense way of dealing with life. He balances me with my analytical-have-to-have perfection approach.

Loren and Brenda

REFLECTION / DIARY

Have you allowed others to influence you in making choices throughout your life? Do you have someone in your life that supports you unconditionally? How did you "move on?"

REFLECTION / DIARY

LETTERS OF SUPPORT

Yea, though I walk through the valley of the shadow of death, I will fear no evil: for thou art with me; thy rod and thy staff they comfort me. Psalm 23:4

~

I am not alone in this experience next you will read letters from women who have dealt with the pain and deception of their husband, lover, child, or relative who's life on the down low was disclosed. The lie is what hurts the most, not the lifestyle.

(Names, geographical, and incriminating information have been changed. If you see yourself in these letters, it is because we are not alone. Someone else shares your same story)

Dear Brenda:

Seeing the impacts of DL brothers everyday:
As a health care professional and a born again believer we are to practice compassions and forgiveness...however, that is difficult to do when sin is not admitted. Many men in the church are living double lives. Christians need to stop turning a blind eye, and call it like it is. Exposure is good! It causes us to DEAL with the issue at hand and not sweep it under the rug. You can love your husband and pray for him, but your life and the well being of your children is at risk! I work in health care...I have seen three married women under 37 years old die from the Down Low Husband. These were beautiful faithful, and GOD fearing women within six months of acknowledging that their worse fears could be true; they were dead, leaving children and family members hurt, confused, and looking for answers. I have some sad stories, but if I can just say one thing more...get tested and do what you need to do in order to LIVE!

***

Your book is astonishing; I finished it in two days. It's great to hear the other side. My husband emphasizes being "truthful" at all times, I couldn't understand why. However, after reading your book I now appreciate the importance of being "truthful," it does set you free. With all the things going on in the world by far the truth is well deserved. Lastly, I must admit you have a beautiful family! Thank you for your guidance, words, and knowledge. Keep up the positive work.

***

To what to do: if you haven't already, pray and follow your heart. You deserve to be happy and in a relationship with a man you trust. Women have to stop closing their eyes and/or looking the other way. HIV/AIDS is a really serious disease. My son died from AIDS complications...he was bisexual. No, his women did not know - and I don't know what has happened to his last lady friend. I have another infected friend...this is NO JOKE. Put yourself first. You cannot change him, he must want to change and then make an effort to stop straddling that fence. But if you are willing to play his game...he has his desires fulfilled on all fronts. What about yours?

***

Thank you for being a voice. I have been married for 28 years to a man I've wondered whether he is on the down low or not. If anybody on the outside was to give an opinion they would say I have a great marriage, and a wonderful family. I just finished reading your book. There are some signs, but not enough other than our sex life or lack of. He has always refused to explain. Yes, he does have a "fishing buddy." That I prohibit from our home. I want out of this, but am afraid (I'm 49). I have a college degree.

***

I recently have experienced accusations about my husband living a down low life style. I just finished your ex-husband books, in just one night, after viewing the BET special. I just learned that you also published a book that I am rushing out to get. His information was and is helpful but I'm in need of hearing from you! Unfortunately my husband still denies what's going on and I still want and love him. As a baptized believer in Christ, and a leader in our church, how am I suppose to use this horrible experience as a testimony, and I'm still dealing with the embarrassment of this test? It's like I don't have anyone to share the hurt and pain with. I wouldn't dare share this with anyone!!

***

After meeting you in Chattanooga and reading your book and seeing your commitment to the cause I will always stand a little taller knowing that women like you are on our side.

***

I did not read your book yet, but I did read coming up from the down low. My son is a teenager. I sometimes think that my son could be gay, I did ask him if he had been with boys, or if he likes boys he said, "yes", but he did not understand. Can you help me?

***

Why are you so hard on J.L.? Aren't you a Christian woman who is supposed to forgive and forget? Are you releasing a book to get back at him?

Because that's what it seems like to me. Let go and Let God. What are your kids saying?

***

I was able read your book I am a woman who was marred to a man on the down low he had aids and gave it to me, from it I gave birth to twins one born with HIV. I want to say, at the time I did not leave. I was young. I had aids and felt death was coming. The pain my husband gave me made me mistrust men, it was not until last year that I learned to trust again. I remarried, but it took time to trust love. My first husband died of aids. He weighed only 30 pounds; seeing him die was hard. At the time I did not know about the down low he was a nice looking man in church but soon he was like, I cannot hide being gay. He made me hate myself, but by God's love I was able start healing even forgive my dead husband. I have had aids for 24 years if I had known he was gay I would not have married him. I wanted to be loved even if it meant being beat I feel women need to learn that: you do not need a man to feel okay. I have learned love God first then self. I need to say your book is healing; you are a person who God has used thank you. You are in my prayers.

***

I am a 30 something year old single mother to three teenage children. I am also a full-time college student with a full time job. I have not had the chance to read your book, but I wanted to let you know that you are doing a good thing. We as black women need a shoulder to lean on in time of need. We go thru life with our heads hanging down, holding so much in, until we think of easy ways to end our lives just because we are hurting, and so full of pain (someone has caused).
I have not experienced what you have, but I have had relationships to go bad for other reasons. I felt that I did not have anyone to talk to, and this was happening only to me.
The Lord does not mean to do anything to hurt us, but things happen for a reason.

***

After reading your ex husband's book all I could say was, wow. There were so many things that as a woman I overlooked when looking at a man. I chose to read his book out of curiosity and now I about to read yours (hopefully in two days also). I want to read yours coming from a woman's point of view. While lying in bed, with my man of two years, I began asking him

questions, laugh out loud. Questions that should have been asked a long time ago, not that I'm having doubts that he's on the DL but just to hear what he had to say.

It made me think of the many times I have "just thrown it out there" with no protection. I feel both books will be a real eye-opener for me and I plan on sharing the books with my friends. Keep up the good work.

***

After reading your book, I was trying to ascertain how to sort out his behavior. Why? Because you stated that he treated you well and yet you kept him with his daily behavior of mistreating you. You were right you called it Dr. Jekyll and Mr. Hyde. I thought, your inner strength, and faith kept you from falling. I have learned while working with humans that one of the greatest things someone can do is to control a human mind. Yes, he was spearing things with you in the marriage, but you had something to sustain you in my view. You would be mentally ill or dead today. I see why you are in a ministry you are giving the glory to the omnipotent, the protecting force of this world. I have always said there is something in this universe that is bigger than you and I, and they control and protect you when you think there is no way out.

***.

I went to a training once for fraud and learned of the behavior of sociopaths: (Dangerous) don't empathize, don't exhibit emotions, no connectedness, no deep feelings, very manipulative, pathological liars, do not except responsibility for behavior; not all are criminal. Some fit your former husband.

***

I really enjoyed reading your book. It is very spirit filled. Thank you for being there to help people.

***

I hope you receive this. I cannot tell l you how much I enjoyed your book. I read it straight through. I am a 47 year-

old black woman who was married to a gay man. I am now in another marriage where I have been abused for 10 years. I am writing, praying, trusting God, and learning to love myself to see what's next for me

***

I have just read your book, and found myself identifying with many parts of it. Thoughts I would like to share with you: It seems that you were brought up in a very religious, upstanding family, and that you may have been a little naive when you married. I was thinking that these guys not only need a cover, as you have said, but they need someone like us, who will not suspect anything, or expect much from them sexually. Perhaps you have already had these thoughts, but I do not remember reading them in the book. I wish you much success and happiness in your new life.

***

I purchased your book and received it today. I have yet to read the entire book. Actually, after reading the book cover I was so amazed. We both are Christian women. What amazed me was how the HOLY SPIRIT was and is operating in our lives. We both have lived the same life style. I was married years before my husband's death due to aids. I have four children. When God be for you who can be against you?

***

Telling your story of survival, healing, reconciliation, and forgiveness will go to places and spaces that James' story will not. And it's a story that needs to be told, and you are the one called to do it. Isn't it amazing what miracles God can make out of the pain and anguish of our lives? The two of you are a wonder to behold. I will keep you in my prayers.

***

You are a brave lady. My daughter bought your ex's book. She is trying to figure out her dad. Good luck.

***

Thank you for writing <u>On The Up and Up</u>. I am young, too young to have gone through all that I went through; I am only 25 soon to be 26. I am white, and my ex-husband is black, and woo wee, he was and is still on the DL.

However, my life experience is so close to yours but yet different in other ways, as you describe the personality differences, I recognized it all from the beginning, which I might add, none of the signs were there until after we were married. So, from the beginning, I mean after, we were married and he started acting strange, which was not even a month after marriage. However, to make himself feel better for his actions he made me think he was cheating on me with women, and he was, but not only women. He is and was so confused about himself and who he is as a person that he would meet people on the Internet pick an argument with me, and that fast he would be out the door. He would usually meet with a man and then a woman, or one night a man and then the next a woman. He was in a constant conquest for trying to figure out what he really wanted, but yet he needed me on the "home front," to keep up the good appearances. I am not the type of woman to find something out and keep it to myself, I wait until I have enough ammunition, then go for it, to make sure I have enough to cover my grounds, and what happened, he tried to kill me, not once but a few times. I ceased having sexual relations with him. I didn't want to possibly get infected. After I left him for the third time and he found me again, I was trying to make peace and would only allow him to see the children while I was around. One night he forced sex and got me pregnant with my third child. I look back and knew the signs then and I tried to do something about it, but the more I tried, the more violent he became. It came to the point that he would just do things to hurt me. Thankfully at the current time he is in state prison for molesting my oldest daughter. Obviously I divorced him, but it wasn't until after he was in jail that I even felt safe enough to file for divorce. There are so many similarities yet there are so many differences in our stories. I remember feeling so alone and like I am the only woman in the world going through this type of thing. Like you I put up the pretty face and the front for those on the outside, until one day I finally came to myself. It has been a long hard rough road for me, and my children.

I seriously from the bottom of my heart thank you for writing your book. God Bless.

***

I read your book and I know God sent you to me. I have been praying for the right answer, or asking God what to do. I've been married almost 35 years to the same man and I know he's DL but he told me that he was not doing it anymore, but I don't believe him there are too many little signs I've been picking up on. I want to leave and start a new life but I'm scared that the kids will hate me for telling about their father. Please help me!

***

REFLECTION

When I began on this journey, I thought it was solely about disclosing the gory details of my catching my man having sex with another man. However, the journey evolved, the test became a testimony that grew into a ministry of healing and forgiveness. I speak to groups and churches and share how I had forgiven Melvin and my ex husband, women and men receive healing from wounds of the heart. I shared my healing from Multiple Sclerosis after I had truly forgiven JL in my heart. I was able to extend my experience to help others to understand that anger and revenge was not their answer, to understand that healing would not happen with anger in their hearts. They first had to acknowledge the their reality, then make a decision to forgive the person that had hurt them. People began to understand that the forgiveness of God required them to forgive others.

In the beginning of my relationship reflection journey, I admitted to my naiveté, and to being clueless to what was going on around me. I was clueless as long as I allowed myself to be; after writing <u>On the Up and Up</u> the book took on a life as a catalyst for truth. People were certain the book would be a tell-all description of JL's physical encounters with men, and a graphic picture of me catching him in the act. It was more of a memoir of my deliverance from a marriage of infidelity, how I overcame that hurt and other obstacles in my life. I knew I was not alone in the journey, which other women also suffered in their marriage and relationships as a result of unspoken infidelity. The adulterous behavior of a man sleeping with another man is no less sinful than a man sleeping with another woman outside of marriage. Women did not need a, blow-by-blow, (no pun intended) graphic description of sexual encounters and escapades. I found that women who had experienced the infidelity of a down low man did not need the details. They wanted answers as to how to handle the grief of a severed relationship, how to handle the "slap in the face" of infidelity, and the destruction of their womanhood. For women who defined themselves through their man they wanted to know: What happens to my family now? Who am I now and how do I pick up the pieces? Should I be tested for HIV/AIDS? How do I know he is on the down low, and should I leave him?

When women ask me what are the signs of a man on the down low, I tell them that the primary signs of a man's infidelity with a man are not much different than when a man is cheating with a woman, and the truth is the pain is the same, the destruction of the relationship and the family is the same. Many times I get the response. "He can not be on the down low, he is married. He has children." My answer is, "And? Are you forgetting about my experience?" I pray that you are empowered by my experience, or someone that you know is empowered by my experience.

"Love others unconditionally."

Brenda Stone Browder

~

Trust in God. John 14:1a

Scriptures to Empower and Comfort

(Ask God for an understanding of these scriptures in your life/circumstances.)

Colossians 3:13
1 Corinthians 6:9-12
1 Corinthians 6:19
1 Corinthians 7:4
1 Corinthians 7:12-17
1 Corinthians 11:11
2 Corinthians 6:14
2 Corinthians 12:9-10
1 Chronicles 4:9-10
Ephesians 1:17-19
Ephesians 2:8-9
Ephesians 4:22-24
Ephesians 4:26
Ephesians 4:31-32
Ephesians 5:15-17
Ephesians 5:25-33
Hebrews 4:13
Hebrews 13:4
Hebrews 4:16
Isaiah 43:18-19
Isaiah 53:5-6
James 1:19-20
James 4:10
Jeremiah 33:3
Jeremiah 29:11
Job 42:2
John 1:12
John 14:1
1 John 1:9
Malachi 3:6a
Matthew 5:31-32
Matthew 6:9
Philippians 4:8

Philippians 4:19
Proverbs 3:5-6
Proverbs 5:15-19
Proverbs 16:2
Proverbs 17:22
Proverbs 18:12
Proverbs 20:22
Proverbs 31:14-18&24
Psalm 17:8-9
Psalm 23:4
Psalm 32:3-5
Psalm 40:1-3
Psalm 34:18
Psalm 46:1
Psalm 51:7
Psalm 51:10-17
Psalm 62:7-8
Psalm 72:12
Psalm 103:3-11
Psalm 142: 1-7
Psalm 147:3
Psalm 139:13-16
Romans 3:23
Romans 6:23
Romans 8:1-2
Romans 8:5-6
Romans 8:28
Romans 10:9
Romans 12:1-2
Romans 12:19
1 Thessalonians 4:3-4
2 Timothy 3:16-17
Titus 2:3-5

Brenda and Loren

Made in the USA
Charleston, SC
21 September 2013